Overcoming Depression – Get Happy Again

The Self-Help Workbook for Understanding Depression, Anxiety and Panic Attacks

[2. Edition]

ISBN – 9781077042414

Contents

Disclaimer

This book contains opinions and ideas of the author and is meant to teach the reader informative and helpful knowledge while being entertaining. The instructions and strategies are possibly not right for every reader and there is no guarantee that they work for everyone. Using this book and implementing the information / recipes therein contained is explicitly your own responsibility and risk. This work with all its contents, does not guarantee correctness, completion, quality or correctness of the provided information. Misinformation or misprints cannot be completely eliminated

Self-Help Guide: Overcome Anxiety, Depression & Panic Attacks

Life is filled with changes. These may include emotional, physical or changes of the mental state. Not all changes are welcomed or easy to accept. In many cases, mental and emotional changes can wreak havoc on your life. Emotional or mental changes may lead one to become depressed, anxious, or to suffer from panic attacks. These are truly uncomfortable feelings that may cause serious withdrawal, illness and even death in severe cases.

Is depression impacting your existence? Do you spend endless days trying to get through the simple things or occurrences in life? Does your life seem out of control? Are you anxious in certain situations? Do you experience panic attacks without warning?

Yes? You have more in common with others among you than you know. Millions facing anxiety or depression. Unfortunately, most feel there's nothing that can be done and never seek help to assist them with the anxiety or depression they have.

To overcome these conditions is to acknowledge that something is wrong. Once you've made the acknowledgement, it's imperative to understand why you are experiencing bouts of anxiety, depression or panic attacks. Next, seek help outside yourself. Understandably it's hard to live with these conditions, and it's not suggested that you face them alone. Speak with trusted friends or family about what you are going through. Finally, seek professional guidance or counsel to assist you with the challenges you face.

It is extremely common for those living with depression or anxiety to feel embarrassed or ashamed. Although common, it is not necessary. There is no timeline or guide book that frees you from the restraints of the condition you are living with. However, initiating the proper steps can help you overcome these feelings and live a life of purpose, content and happiness. Your comfort zone is much broader than you know. It's the negative feelings that are holding you down or preventing you from enjoying the marvelous journey that life guides you through.

Are you fed up with depression? Are you tired of spending endless days trying to cope with the simple things or occurrences in life? Are you eager to resume the life you love? Are you eager to overcome sudden anxiety? Are you ready to put those panic attacks to rest?

If you answered yes to one or more of the above questions, this self-guide to overcoming depression, anxiety and panic attacks is for you. You will be given important tools to help you understand, overcome and live. You will grasp the concept of what's taking place in your life that is causing you to experience the feelings you have. You will overcome the obstacles or challenges that destroy your mental or emotional clarity. You will live a life filled with content and purpose without regret. These are unique changes for anyone dealing with depression or anxiety to undergo. You will learn to control the when, how, where and why in your life.

What Is Depression?

The clinical definition of depression is easier explained by identifying the effects it causes on someone's life. The feelings may be different but they all fall under a category of sadness. Living with depression can ultimately impact your ability to function in society. It impedes on your capability to rest, socialize, work, and otherwise lead a normal life.

There are an abundance of causes behind the feelings of depression. If you are or have experienced a major life change you could possibly feel differently, saddened most often. This could be the demise of someone you know or love, loss of a job or a medical diagnosis that changes your life forever. These are just a few of the instances that could cause an onset of your depression.

Don't spend another minute or day waiting to feel better. It doesn't just happen. You must be proactive in seeking help and change. Your happiness and well-being depends on you and the guidance you seek. Your next move to overcome your issues will be a positive one and it will lead to a happier and healthier you.

People who live with depression often find it difficult to do things they once did with ease. It may be something that you found joy in doing and all of a sudden, it is almost impossible for you to do it now. You may feel a sense of loneliness, sadness, defeat and many other inexpressible feelings. This is just a sample of the emotions that those living with depression may encounter. Depression is a condition of the mind, heart and soul because it can affect them all. Your depression may look and feel entirely different from the depression of someone else. It has no face. There are no red flags that protrude from the head. Instead, it is identified by observing the acts and feelings of someone dealing with depression or anxiety, even if you must observed yourself.

Recognizing the Signs or Impacts of Depression

You may be or know someone battling depression but don't know the signs. It is hard to suggest that someone gets help if you aren't sure of the trials they are facing. In order to recognize depression, it helps to know the signs it presents or the changes it causes in one's life.

Once the signs are recognized, you should suggest or encourage help or counseling. Among the most familiar indicators of depression.

- Crying unexplainably or without reason
- Increased or extended periods of sadness
- Excessive anger, aggravation or anxiety
- Cynicism
- Lack of motivation or depleted energy
- Exhaustion without reason
- Battling guilt or lack of self-worth
- Find it difficult to remain focused or make decisions
- No longer interested in things once enjoyed
- Consistent pains or unexplainable aches
- Repetitive thoughts of ending your life

If you experience or know someone who displays signs or symptoms as those stated above, it is likely that they are coping with depression. Once the signs have been recognized, it is time to intervene or seek help. You likely don't know what you should do or where to turn to for help. There are several resources available for people battling this issue.

Consider the following:

☐ Contact your local mental health office

☐ Conduct an online search for counselors or private practice mental health care providers
☐ Speak with others you know who have overcome or are coping with depression

The following table will help you to distinguish between depression and just a bad day. While most people living with depression may appear to just be having an off day, continuous or consistent bad days are an underlying problem that must be faced.

A Bad Day	Depression
Had a bad night and can't get out of bed	Every day is bad and you lay around all day
Lost your job and it is hard finding strength to find another one	Lost your job over a year ago and can't seem to do anything but sleep and cry
Don't have anything to wear to an event so you decide to just stay home	Not interested in attending an event ever and always decline or ignore the invitation
Loss of appetite because you've got so many things that require your attention	Difficulty eating at all because you're facing too many challenges in life
Can't sleep because you depended on caffeine to get you through the hectic day	Most nights are sleepless and you have no idea why but days are spent sleeping in
Feeling guilty because you missed your best friend's birthday	Feeling guilty but not sure why and can't seem to overcome the feeling
Crying because you lost your pet or suffered another sentimental loss	Crying when you wake-up, fall asleep or at any point of the day for no reason at all

What happens once the signs are recognized? What

happens now and better yet, what do you do next? The answers depend on the stage of depression being experienced. At the onset of depression, it may be easier to overcome the challenges it presents. This is primarily because it is the beginning of a bad situation or the trauma is new. In any case, recognition of depression and taking proactive measures to defeat it may be much easier in the beginning.

If you or a loved one is just beginning to feel or exhibit the signs of depression, there are steps you can take immediately. The first step is to take care of yourself or encourage the depressed person to do the same. This doesn't necessarily require a change in medical schedule or for you to work out more often. While both may be necessary, they are not the only things that need to be done. Consider introducing a lifestyle of self-preservation. This allows those dealing with depression to preserve a life of healthiness, happiness and longevity. At this point, you will acknowledge the things you need most to live happily and do what it takes to make them happen. Engage or participate in activities that distract you from things that make you feel sad or anything that promotes a positive approach to a sound mind and puts you at peace each day.

Feelings of depression are more often overcome by connecting with your happy place. This is not necessarily a physical location but sometimes located within. To experience happiness, you may only need to do something that makes you smile or feel great about yourself. The worst part is it's not simple to accomplish, because you may have no idea where to start or what must be done to achieve happiness.

The following activity chart can be helpful in teaching you to separate your day into various feel-good activities.

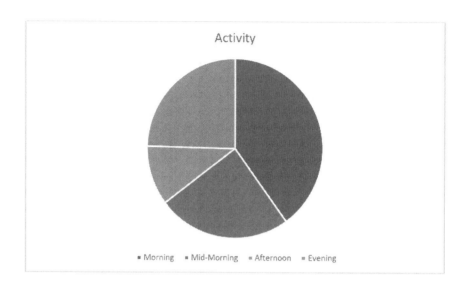

Activity

■ Morning ■ Mid-Morning ■ Afternoon ■ Evening

Morning – Morning time will be the most important aspect of your day, as it establishes the climate for the remainder of your day. Once you awake, take a moment to assess your true feelings. Get in touch with them and find out why you have them. Meditate, enjoy a cup of coffee, tea or water. Listen to your favorite music and make a commitment to make the most of whatever the day throws your way. Allow yourself enough time to do yoga or another fun and relaxing exercise. Make mornings all your own by cooking breakfast, juicing or trying a new recipe. Before leaving home, look in the mirror and say out loud at least three things you like about that person staring back at you. Next, say two things out loud that you think you should change about the person staring back at you.

Mid-Morning – Mid-morning is an important time of day for those dealing with depression. This is typically the time you will begin to think of all the things that are going wrong in your life. It's usually this time of day that you encounter others and begin comparing yourself to those around you. STOP! Remember those positive things that you said you admired about yourself before you left home. Don't focus on others and what they are doing but begin to think of ways you can change the things you don't like about yourself. These are the things that matter most but be sure to not pressure yourself. There are 24-hours in a day and what you don't accomplish or change today, you can start again tomorrow.

Afternoon – Afternoons should be used for refuel sessions. Take the time to reenergize or replenish your happiness. Take a stroll through your favorite neighborhood or park. Visit your favorite coffee house or lunch spot. Spend the afternoon reading to kids in a library or local school. These are things or activities that remind you of how much of an essential asset you are in the life of your own and others

Evening – Evening is the best time of day to put your feelings on the shelf. Shut down any negative events that took place during the day. Don't take anything that happened personally and most importantly, don't allow bad situations or occurrences to make you feel less than valuable. Reassess whatever happened during the day and move forward with your evening without dwelling on those times. It may help to tell yourself that you will deal with what you can, when you can. Once the work or school day is over, it's time to just be happy. Schedule an evening out with friends, take in a movie by yourself, attend a concert or enjoy a movie night at home. Long relaxing baths and soothing music are great for ending any kind of day and can help you to relax and sleep better at night.

*Notice that the largest areas of the day are morning and evening. It is because these are the most important times of day for setting and resetting your emotions and feelings. Give these hours considerable time and consideration to help you feel your absolute best each day.

The Stages of Depression

You should try and understand that medical professionals do not acknowledge or assign stages to depression. Keep in mind, the common process of progression that a large category of people identify as stages. Prior to noticing any bodily changes, your thoughts and emotions begin to change. It is common to begin blaming yourself for things that are not your fault or feeling despondent about issues or challenges you are facing in life. Pacing the floor, eating less or not at all and staying up into all hours of the night are common occurrences.

The process or stages as some call them of depression may appear as follows:

Observation – this is the stage where you begin to wonder if depression is the case and what life issues are causing the depression. You begin to observe the changes and identify the symptoms.

Preparation – this stage is where you may speak to someone about the thoughts or feelings you have. You begin to research articles or read self-help guides to see what is happening in your life.

Proactive- this stage begins when you step up and take action. Make an appointment with a health care professional or counselor to seek a professional diagnosis. You may be prescribed medication or begin therapeutic exercises. These measures help to encourage relaxation and relive stress.

How You Feel

Once depression hits, you begin to feel a combination

of mixed emotions. You will experience a sense of disconnect from the world, extreme loneliness and a loss of energy or motivation. It helps to communicate or talk to others, forge happy and healthy relationships with your support systems and surround yourself with people or things that make you feel happy and appreciated. These are all positive steps to help battle depression. However, no one expects you to be with someone or depend on others all the time. Therefore, it is imperative that you learn to engage in activities alone without feeling sad or depressed.

Consider the following suggestions to help you enjoy your alone time.

Get Active

Depression can make you feel drained and cause you to lose interest in almost all physical activities. Make a commitment to spend at least thirty minutes per day being active. Ride a bike, throw a ball to your dog in the park, sign-up for a dance class or some other type of physical activity you would enjoy. Professionals suggest that participating in consistent exercises does wonders for your emotional and mental mood. It also helps to alleviate signs of depression that many adults experience. The endorphins that are released during active exercises contribute to mood enhancement and helps to decrease symptoms of depression.

Relax

Most people dealing with depression spend a large part of their day feeling stressed or worried about things beyond their control. It's time to relax. Meditation is a great resource when seeking a relaxed state of mind and body. It disturbs the negative thought pattern. There are several types of meditation that include traditional and contemporary options. You may consider signing up for a class or if it's more comfortable, follow a meditation expert on television or a YouTube video.

Adopt a Pet

Pets give just as much love as they require. They are great in helping people overcome feelings of depression or loneliness. Caring for a pet will make you feel responsible and in charge. If you have been battling depression, begin with an animal that requires little attention. This will prevent feelings of guilt from settling in if you fail to walk the dog, trim the cat and other responsibilities on a regular schedule. Pets or animals will help bring a sense of fulfillment to your life.

Become a Volunteer

You will find that it feels great to give of your time where others need it most. Become a volunteer in your community, school or at work. Volunteering delivers a feeling of satisfaction and creates structure in an otherwise unorganized lifestyle. You will begin to see how your efforts are needed and appreciated by others, which makes you feel good or better about yourself. You can volunteer as little as two-five hours per month and begin to see the difference in how you feel. It helps to keep it light and not make it feel like an obligation.

Join a Book Club

Do you enjoy reading? Books are a great way to engage your inner happiness. Join a book club to discuss a good book with others who have similar interests as yourself. If you prefer to read alone, pick up a motivational or inspirational book. Regardless if you are reading for self-improvement or pleasure. It's critical that you engage in a storyline that shifts your mood and encourages positive emotions.

Turn Up the Music

Do you enjoy music and dancing? Perhaps you have a favorite artist or group that you haven't listened to in a while. Download a few of your favorite songs and listen to them at any time you're feeling down. Dance around to one or more of your favorite songs. It's okay to dance in the park or even in the rain. The point is to turn up the music, nod your head or dance the night away.

How Depression Impacts Your Body

Depression can alter your physical composition, just as it does your emotional state. Long before it becomes too bad, your body may begin to exhibit signs that it is being impacted by depression. Signs may exist temporarily or long-term as the result of a traumatic experience. If you have been experiencing prolonged feelings of sadness for longer than two or three weeks, it could be a sign of severe depression. Other conditions associated with the signs that present themselves during depression are Post-Traumatic Stress Disorder (PTSD) or bipolar disorder. While the latter are both very serious illnesses, depression can be identified by a few common symptoms as those previously listed.

Depression is diagnosed in a person that exhibits five or more of these signs for two or more consecutive weeks.

Mood is sad or feeling defeated most days	Tired or exhaustion without reason
Unable to enjoy favorite activities	Excessive or lack of sleep
Extreme weight loss	Extreme weight gain
Diminished self-worth	Having a hard time completing tasks
Lingering thoughts of suicide	Isolation from others are being withdrawn

You should know that depression impacts not only your life, but the life of those around you as well. It can begin to cause changes in important relationships at home, work, and in your social circle. How has depression caused your life to change? Maybe changes have occurred and you're not aware that depression is the cause.

Sufferers of depression may also experience the following impacts on their body.

If you or someone you know has begun to experience unexplainable feelings, emotions and changes within the human physique, depression could be the cause. It is important to seek help before these conditions lead to more severe, life-threatening episodes. The way your body reacts to your emotions has a huge impact on its performance. Take the initiative to undergo regular mental and physical check-ups to sustain your happiness and well-being.

The Various Categories of Depression

The signs and symptoms of depression may seem easy enough to identify but there are various categories to help assess the severity of the condition. You may hear the term depression and immediately think of clinical or ordinary depression. The initial requiring professional treatment and the other is a common type that almost anyone can experience from time to time. These are both common but not specific categories. It is most difficult to categorize depression because it is usually referenced as a symptom and a condition. Confusing, right?

Your thoughts and feelings are severely impacted by depression, which makes it challenging to live a normal life. There are several contributing factors that lead to depression, and some are still very unclear.

Have a look at some of the most common categories of the condition.

1. **Major Depression**

Major depression is one that typically requires medical or professional treatment. This is usually referenced to as DD (major depressive disorder). This group may be categorized by several key factors:

- Mood disorder

- Loss of interest in well-liked activities
- Fluctuation in weight
- Abnormal sleep pattern
- Exhaustion
- Loss of self-value
- Inability to focus

2. Persistent Disorder of Depression

Otherwise categorized as Dysthymia, persistent depression is a type that may exist for up to two years. The condition can be one that is mild to extreme.

3. Bipolar Depression

This category of depression is best described by stages of atypically heightened mood called mania. They can be mild or extenuating resulting in dominant impairment of one's life, which sometimes causes hospitalization or loss of realistic thoughts and actions. Those experiencing bipolar disorder might have major depression.

There are a large group of physical and sensitive signs that occur with this type depression including:

- Frustration and anxiety
- Unexplainable and constant aches and inflammation
- Decreased self-esteem
- Unusual lack of organization
- Lethargy and sleep pattern changes

4. Postpartum

Motherhood is a beautiful experience but it can cause an emotional toll on the mother. Hormones change during pregnancy and may negatively impact the mother's mood. This could possibly lead to a period of depression. Most commonly, the mom will experience obstinate lethargy and feelings of sadness. It is always recommended that mothers seek medical or professional guidance during this category of depression. Left untreated, postpartum could lead to more severe occurrences such as delusions or confusion.

5. Atypical

Do you find yourself depressed which leads to eating more than usual, sleeping a lot more than normal, or sensitive to things not going your way but instantly happy when a positive activity or big event takes place?

This describes atypical types of depression. It is associated with a particular category of symptoms:

- Robust sensitive moods
- Extremely sensitive to refutation
- Feeling overwhelmed
- Unwarranted sleep
- Extreme food intake

People who experience atypical type of depression generally respond well to prescription antidepressants.

Feeling Blue? Could It Be Depression? Take the Quiz to See If Depression Is Effecting You!

Are you or someone you know displaying signs or symptoms of depression. Take the following quiz to determine if depression is the problem.

1. Getting to Sleep

   o Takes less than thirty-minutes
   o Occasionally but not often takes up to thirty-minutes or more to drift off to sleep
   o Usually takes half an hour or longer to drift off to sleep
   o Always take longer than thirty-minutes to drift off to sleep

2. Each Night

   o I sleep throughout the night
   o I am restless at night and sometimes wake up because I sleep lightly
   o I will awake once during sleep, but fall back asleep with ease
   o I often wake up throughout the night for at least half an hour

3. Daily Wake-Up

   o Usually, I wake-up a half-hour or less before time to rise
   o Usually, I wake-up forty-five minutes or later before the time to rise
   o I often wake-up at least an hour or more before needed but can fall back asleep with ease
   o I often wake-up at least an hour or more before needed and have trouble falling back asleep

4. Amount of Sleep

- o I usually sleep no more than seven or eight hours each night with no daytime nap
- o I usually sleep a maximum of ten hours within a full day including any brief or prolonged naps
- o I usually sleep a maximum of twelve hours within a full day including any brief or prolonged naps
- o I usually sleep more than twelve hours within a full day including some time towards naps

5. How Do You Feel?

- o You never feel sad
- o You occasionally experience feelings of sadness
- o You usually experience feelings of sadness
- o You are sad almost each day

6. Eating Habits

- o My appetite has not changed
- o My appetite has left and is not the same
- o My appetite has increased and I'm eating a lot more than usual

7. Loss of Appetite

- o I occasionally eat less than usual
- o I don't eat often and when I do I must force myself
- o I seldom eat within a day and then I must make myself eat or be encouraged by others

8a. Weight Changes

- o My weight has not changed
- o I have experienced weight loss
- o I have experienced weight gain

8b. Weight Drop

- o I may have experienced some weight loss
- o I have lost at least two pounds
- o I have lost at least five pounds

*If your answers to the above questions indicate significant change compared to the way you normally do things or how you normally exist, you may be experiencing mild to moderate depression. Depression isn't a feeling that has to describe your entire life. You may feel better soon with effort and if not, seeking professional guidance should be the next step.

Where to Seek Help When Depressed

It can be extremely hard to talk about your feelings of depression. However, choosing to ignore them can result in more severe problems. If there are no friends, family or any other person that you can reach out and communicate with, there is an abundance of resources available for your convenience. The problem most people have is determining who or where to turn to for help.

Below are resources that help with depression.

Support Groups or Helplines appear in your local phone directory or online

Medical or Counseling Centers for Mental Disorders

Suicide Prevention Hotline

How Depression Can Change Your Life

The fact that depression can occur at almost any age makes it possible to slightly or drastically change your life. It can be overwhelming living with constant changes in habits, lifestyle and daily activities. Many times it causes mass confusion within and among friends or family. You are familiar with the way you typically do things but all of a sudden, you do them differently.

These type changes can make you wonder what to do next or when things will return to normal. More importantly, it can make you feel that you've lost complete control of your life and need to do something to regain that control.

You may have difficulty eating, sleeping or simply breathing. The breathing issues may be signs of panic attacks that are sometimes caused by depression. Your school work may begin to diminish or you may begin to fall behind at work. In addition, you may begin to notice that your relationships aren't as healthy and you can't focus like you did at one time. Alcoholism and drug addiction will sometimes accompany depression. You will notice that depression is wide-spread, meaning it also affects those around you. If gone untreated, you may experience difficulties in your social and professional circles. Therefore, you should move forward and seek professional counsel.

Doing so brings a standard of quality not only to some areas of your life but also to your peace of mind.

Depression and Your Work

Chances are that if you work, you either love or need your job. Either way, positive productivity is necessary. It is easy for depression to creep up and change your performance or production in the workplace. This happens often without warning. Many people who are living with depression may not be aware that their work is suffering or that there has been any changes in their behavior.

Here are signs that your work may be suffering due to depression.

- You are calling off more than usual for no valid reason
- You find yourself drifting off while working and thinking of everything except work
- Your productivity is down
- You no longer engage or connect with your co-workers
- You make constant errors of judgement at work

How can you improve these conditions or feelings to prevent work from becoming or burden or worse, in jeopardy?

- Put forth extra effort to report to work and don't call off if there is not good reason
- Consider the task itself and leave non-work related issues outside of work
- Keep track of your productivity and perform consistent updates to ensure you are on track
- Communicate with your co-workers at least once daily

- Double check your work to ensure that mistakes are minimum

Depression and Your School Work

School work can be overwhelming at any time but especially during periods of depression. If you fall behind in school work, it can be difficult to catch up and maybe impossible to do so at times. You don't have to deny your condition or delay treatment. It helps to act immediately if you are experiencing moments of depression. Once grades begin to decline or interest in studies become almost non-existent, it may be too late.

Here are signs that your school work may be suffering due to depression.

- You are missing class more often
- You are not attentive in class
- You don't put forth an effort to study for tests
- Your grades have gotten bad
- You have little or no interest in your education

How can you improve these conditions to prevent school work from suffering?

- Attend class even when if it's the last thing you wish to do
- Pay attention in class
- Take good notes and study prior to exams
- Work to keep your grades in good standing
- Recall the reasons you seek or desire an education and how it will improve your life

Depression and Your Social Life

Your social life can take a big hit when depression comes into the picture. You begin to feel withdrawn and desire isolation. It is almost impossible for some depressed people to pull themselves out of bed, much less mingle or associate with others. It seems that when dealing with depression, it's hard to resume or maintain social activities. Your interest isn't there and feelings of low self-esteem make it hard to be around people most of the time. Once you remove yourself from friends, family or coworkers, it's likely that depression has had an impact on your social life. You shouldn't allow this to go on for extensive periods of time, as it can lead to damaged or destroyed relationships.

Here are signs that your social life may be suffering due to depression.

- You decline or ignore social invites
- You ignore calls or visits from friends, family or loved ones
- You put forth no effort to socialize or participate in social activities
- Your days are spent alone
- You have no desire to leave home if not absolutely necessary

How can you improve these feelings to prevent your social life from suffering?

- Accept at least one social invite per month
- Take at least two or more calls from friends and return texts by the end of day
- Strive to be social or mingle with friends

- Spend at least two hours each day with family or friends
- Get out and exercise or take a walk daily

Coping With Depression

Depression doesn't have to get the best of you or control your life. It does require you to take a few important steps to get ahead of the challenges it presents. To begin, seek professional counsel. You can speak with friends and family for support but only a professional can diagnose and treat you properly. In addition to professional care, you should be proactive in your coping techniques. Not everyone will respond the same to self-help, but the following could help decrease or alleviate symptoms that may appear.

Tips for Dealing with Depression

In addition, these steps are iatrical in providing you the needed strength to manage daily living and to eliminate factors that place your mental well-being at risk.

Physical Activities

Physical activity gives your body the strength it needs to sustain from day to day. Research indicates that physical activities ignite positive chemicals that works to enhance mood.

There are several available methods to stay or introduce activity into your lifestyle. Regardless of your physical state or desire, finding exercises to incorporate into your day to day can be enjoyable and useful. Consider activities such as yoga, Zumba, running, swimming or cycling. If you desire or require something easier, consider walking or jogging at a slow pace. You can incorporate exercise into your daily routine by parking farther away from the entrance, walking the dog to the park that's further away from home or walking to the shopping center or work.

Try to incorporate at least one to two hours of physical activity per week. Keep track of activities that elevate your heart rate and engage all the muscles of the body.

Eat Well

Eating a healthy and well-balanced diet is important at all times, but especially when coping with depression. The energy obtained from food serves as fuel for your mental and physical state.

It is common for most to intake three meals and one

to two light snacks per day. A healthy diet consists of lean proteins, fresh veggies and fruits, whole grains and low-fat dairy. The consumption of healthy and nutritious foods makes you feel great throughout the day. Avoid pre-packaged foods when possible and consider gardening when possible to keep fresh foods nearby and easily accessible.

You need to hydrate by drinking sufficient amounts of water. It's easy to determine how much water you should take in. Simply divide your weight by two and drink that amount in ounces each day.

Rest Well

A good night's rest is an essential element in leading a healthy and fulfilled life. Sleep recharges the body and helps it to prepare for the next day. The brain begins to feel cluttered and fatigued without efficient amounts of sleep. Eight to ten hours each night is the suggested amount for teenagers. Most adults can thrive on seven to eight hours of sleep each night. It may be challenging to get the necessary amount of sleep, especially when depressed.

Begin by making the area you sleep in relaxing. Try falling asleep in a cool room with dim or dark lights. You may need to add blinds or shades to the window to decrease light interference. Consider sleeping with ear plugs, a fan and comfortable pillows and bedding. The hour prior to retiring for the night should be a relaxed one. Put down the phone, homework or work that you brought home from the office. Drink water if thirsty and avoid caffeine within that hour also. Avoid spicy foods and sugary snacks.

Wondering what can help you unwind if you have to say no to all your feel-good things? Take a soak in the tub or warm shower. Read your favorite novel or motivational guide. Sip on warm tea or milk and listen to soft music before bed. These are great ways to prepare your body mentally and physically for a good night's rest.

Address Any Issues With Your Health

Your emotional state improves when you tackle health issues head-on. You feel better because you've taken the initiative to take care of yourself. Many people who live with unaddressed health issues worry endlessly about what could be wrong or what may happen. Research indicates that there is an association between unaddressed health issues and feelings of depression, specifically inflammatory ailments. Taking care of health concerns could work to enhance your mood because you're not dealing with constant pain and other illnesses.

Stay Away From Unsafe Substances

Coping with stress is never easy. There are positive and negative ways to deal with factors that lead to stress. A negative approach includes taking part in activities that may enhance your mood at the moment but will eventually leave you feeling down. These activities include but aren't limited to the use of illegal drugs, abuse of alcohol and exhibiting dangerous behaviors such as cutting or huffing.

Exist In the Moment

Stay in tune with your mind and inner-peace. When overwhelm sets in, it's easy to focus on past issues or things that are going on in the background. These thoughts can cause feelings of depression and unjust stress. Existing in the moment encourages you to free your mind of anything negative, which helps you to concentrate on your happiness in that moment. This existence should take place when you are with friends, family or alone.

Practice S.I.T.E.

Before your day begins, at the climax of your day, while traveling home, in the shower or before falling asleep, initiate F.I.T.E.

Freeze and stop doing whatever you're doing for a moment.

Inhale. Breathe as usual and take natural breaths in and out the nose.

Think clearly. Actually ponder your thoughts. Assess what they mean. Acknowledge and accept whatever you observe. Focus on your mind, body and any physical perceptions you experience during this time. Notice if your heart races, muscles tighten or pain sets in.

Exercise anything that supports you at this very moment. It may be speaking with family or friends or stretching before bed.

Proceed With Love

This may sound easy but most people coping with depression find it extremely difficult. The requirements of school, work and family can make it difficult to approach or do the things we actually love to do. Engage in activities that enhance your life. Paint, dance, volunteer or bake a cake. Whatever brings you joy, do it!

Tips to Help You Cope with Depression

You should work to discover ways to help you cope with depression. This is a powerful coping mechanism that assists you in working through the daily spurts of feeling down and overwhelmed. There are effective ways to cope with emotional, mental and physical setbacks. One extremely effective approach is exercise because it gets you up and moving. It is also a beneficial tool in helping to clear your mind of random or oppressive thoughts.

Elevated mood is one of the most impactful strategies or techniques utilized to cope with disorders such as anxiety. You may consider adopting a regular exercise regimen, scheduling a weekly connect with a current or old friend or taking a class to learn something new. These are merely ideas that may work in getting you through the coping process. Effective coping helps you to remove the fog that clouds your mind, judgement and feelings. It results in a happy and extremely outgoing lifestyle that makes each day worth celebrating.

Below are additional strategies or suggestions to help cope with depression.

Don't Abandon Your Support System

Depression will make you feel that you have no one around who is willing to help. This is common when dealing with low self-esteem. While your days may be spent in isolation and feeling lonely, you are not alone. There are friends and family who want you to be happy again. It is challenging to battle depression alone. You likely feel ashamed or embarrassed about neglecting friends or family, but you should put these feelings to rest. Connect with your social circle and family to enhance your mood. This will do wonders for you. You will discover that communicating with those who care about you and your well-being instills a sense of renewed strength within you.

If you feel alone and think there is no one to lean on, establish new relationships to strengthen your bridge of support.

Utilizing these suggestions may help you to stay connected.

- **Seek support from those who encourage you to be who you truly are.** The goal isn't to find someone who can make you better. You just need someone who will lend a listening ear. This person should be understanding, compassionate and sensitive to what you're feeling.
- **Arrange a face –to-face.** It's always a great idea to text or get a phone call but nothing is better than face-to-face interaction. Facial expressions are iatrical in expressing and understanding the struggles or challenges a person is facing. Talk it over and feel relief in no time because you have connected with someone who cares about your issues.
- **Mend your social butterfly wing.** At one time you were the social butterfly, but depression has caused one of your wings to become damaged. Get out and mingle, even when your mind and body is telling you not to do so. It helps to associate with others in that it puts your mind on positive things and helps to relieve your feelings of depression.
- **Be someone's support system.** You like to feel supported and should offer that same support to others. This is a great mood enhancer in that it helps you to feel good about yourself when helping others. Listen to someone else's problem

or volunteer to help the less fortunate. You feel different when you know that what you're doing or who you are is making a difference.

- **Find a support channel.** It may be helpful to speak with others who are dealing with depression. It helps you to feel less isolated and presents an opportunity for you to be encouraged and offer encouragement to others.

Tips to Stay In Touch With Your Support Outlet

1. Choose at least one person to discuss what you're going through
2. Help others with their issues
3. Meet a friend for coffee or a movie
4. Have a friend or co-worker check in on you occasionally
5. Join someone for a social outing
6. Reach out to an old friend
7. Choose a workout partner
8. Arrange weekly lunch or dinner outings
9. Join a class to see new faces
10. Speak with a counselor, clergy or therapist

Reconnect With Things You Enjoy

To effectively battle depression, you must reconnect with enjoyable things and make you feel energized. Examples include practicing healthy living, effectively managing overwhelming situations, doing only the things you feel you can achieve and adding enjoyable activities to your daily routine.

Do Something You Enjoy. Although it may be challenging to do so while feeling depressed, you must motivate yourself to do something you enjoy or at one time found exciting to do. Getting up and going out to do your favorite things can make you feel happy and accomplished. It may not be an immediate relief to your depression but it will help to capitalize on our positive feelings at the moment. Revisit an old hobby or activity you once enjoyed. Connect with your creative side by engaging in music, dance, art or theater. Visit a park or museum.

Become Health Conscious. Become aware of your health by first, ***getting enough rest***. If depression is an issue, chances are, you're losing or getting too much sleep. Adapt a health schedule that enables a rejuvenated feeling when you awake.

Alleviate stress wherever possible. Stress is a primary contributor to depression. It acts as a trigger and causes it to become worse over time. Identify the elements in your life that trigger your stress meter and define ways to eliminate it and get a grasp on your life.

Calming Techniques. Practice techniques or strategies that help you to feel relaxed. Relaxation is a key tool to relieving and eliminating stress and depression. Suggestions for calming exercises include meditation, muscle engagement and yoga.

Here is a "happiness toolkit" to help you battle depression.

1. Get out and embrace nature
2. Make a list of things you love about yourself
3. Choose a book to read each month
4. Enjoy a funny sitcom or movie
5. Enjoy a nice warm bubble bath

6. Tackle a few small chores
7. Visit or volunteer at the animal shelter
8. Talk with friends in person
9. Turn up the music and dance
10. Make a spontaneous decision to do something different

Move Around

As simple as it sounds, people living with depression find it extremely difficult to just move around. Getting out of bed, exiting the vehicle, getting out of their own way, and getting out of the house is simply hard to accomplish when depressed. Adopting an active lifestyle is a critical weapon in the fight against depression. According to research, exercise is equally beneficial in dealing with depression as medication may be. Commit to participate in exercise or some type of physical activity for at least half-an-hour per day. You can break the time up into increments or do it all at once. Just figure out how to be more active each day.

Exercise is a Mood Enhancer

You will feel less fatigued. In the beginning it may be hard but eventually, your fatigue will become less with exercise or physical activity. Increased energy levels are primary mood enhancers.

Stay in rhythm. Participate in exercises or activities that are consistent and rhythmic, as they are great for battling depression. Consider walking, dancing, weight class or swimming, as these all engage both the upper and lower extremities.

Engage your feelings. If you are depressed because of a traumatic experience, get in touch with how your body responds or reacts to movement. Notice the little things like the moment your foot touches the ground, how lightly the wind hits your cheek or your breathing patterns.

Get Sun-Kissed

Sunlight delivers a healthy dose of Vitamin D, and the D is not for depression. Sunshine helps to elevate levels of serotonin, which stimulates the mood. Take in 15-20 minutes of sunlight each day. Use sunscreen when necessary and never gaze directly into the sunlight.

Here are ways to connect with sunlight.

- Enjoy a lunchtime walk, sip your coffee on the deck or eat lunch on the patio
- Get moving outside instead of in a gym or in front of the television. Play tennis or hike a trail to enjoy nature while soaking in the sun.
- Allow more natural sunlight inside your house by raising the blinds or peeling back the drapes of the windows.
- If sunshine is not frequent in your area, consider light therapy techniques or boxes

Combat Negative Thoughts

Are you feeling day after day feeling vulnerable or powerless? Are you thinking that you're in a hopeless situation and there's nothing you can do to change it? Depression has the tendency to creep into your mind and make every thought you generate a negative one. You begin to think negatively about yourself and everything you encounter.

These negative thought associations are not okay. Don't allow them to manipulate or overwhelm your existence. It won't be easy to terminate the negative thoughts, but it is possible. Each time a negative thought enters your mind, extinguish it with a positive twist to the thought. You'll be creating a balance in your thought process and alleviating in negativity that exists.

Negative Thoughts That Give Depression Power Over Your Life

Establish a middle-ground. Your thought process doesn't have to be all or nothing. You don't have to get every answer correct and there is room for error in every decision you make. Acknowledge this and be okay with it.

One negative result doesn't defy the person you really are. Don't allow a single idea or action that went wrong in your life to define you. It's no indication that everything else will fail. More importantly, it doesn't make you a failure.

Erase the negative over positive mentality. Depression will make you overlook every positive thing that goes right in your life and cause you to focus only on the negative. Think of all the good and positive things that happen to you. These will by far outweigh the negative.

Stop drawing conclusions without proof or facts. You are ruining your life by always assuming you can predict the outcome of things. You have no idea the length of time it will take you to finish school. The point is that you must begin somewhere. It doesn't matter how long it takes you as long as you finish.

Emotional nonsense. Your feelings of defeat or failure are nonsense. You spend day after day telling yourself that you are a failure or not good at anything. You are the only person that feels this way and without reason, it's only your depressed emotions that make you think so.

The "I Can't" syndrome. Stop telling yourself that you can't do something that you've not attempted. The category of your desired things to do is the starting list of things that can be done if you are proactive in making them happen.

Get Out of the Box. You cannot remain isolated or enclosed inside a box because of previous or past mistakes. Stop calling yourself a failure or worthless. You're neither of those things.

Give Your Negative Connotations the Third-Degree

Once the negative thought patterns that live inside your head have been identified, it's time to bring them in for questioning. Ask yourself:

- What facts or proof make this or these thoughts have substance? No substance?
- What would I advise a loved one or friend who thought this way?
- Can I look at this from another perspective or is there another reason that this has happened?
- How would I view this if depression weren't involved?

Giving your negative encounters the third degree will cause them to lose value and diminish rather quickly. In the meantime, you will establish a more level perspective and help defeat the depression you have.

Time to Seek Help

Once you've completed the process of self-help and remain faithful to the positive changes your life needs, if you find that your depression is not better, you should seek professional guidance. This is no indication of weakness. It only means that you're in sync with your feelings and emotions enough to know that you can't and don't have to endure the process on your own.

The above coping techniques are beneficial and pair effectively with the professional help you seek.

Exercises to Help You Feel Better When Depression Strikes

Depression will change the way you view life in almost every perspective. It causes mental and physical fatigue that interferes with your social and professional existence. Depression is not something anyone wants to endure. It contributes tremendously to low self-esteem, diminished health and happiness as a whole.

- Do you dread waking up in the mornings?
- Do you dread spending days alone?
- Are you tired of feeling lonely and depressed?
- Do you experience frequent headaches and don't know why?
- Are you afraid to express yourself because you feel that you have no valuable contribution to offer?
- Is your life different and less fulfilled than it once was?
- Are you having difficulty eating or tolerating your favorite foods?
- Do you separate yourself from others because you feel different or ashamed about something?

If your answers to three or more of the above questions are yes, you need to take proactive steps to battle and defeat depression. It can consume your life, but only if you allow it to do so.

Daily Steps

	Morning	Noon	Evening
Monday	Meditation	Have lunch outside	Paint or draw a picture
Tuesday	Yoga	Visit a new restaurant for lunch	Create a playlist
Wednesday	Morning Walk	Take an afternoon walk	Listen to your playlist
Thursday	Coffee with a Friend	Go to a museum	Rearrange a space in your home
Friday	Dance in the Mirror	Take a friend to lunch	Take a different route home
Saturday	Go Thrifting	Treat yourself to a spa day (nails, hair, massage)	Go out with friends
Sunday	Declare Affirmations	Bake a dessert for dinner	Take an evening stroll

It is important that you take the necessary steps daily to defeat depression or to reduce the impact that it has on your life.

Daily Defeat of Negativity

The process to defeat negativity is one that must be repeated daily. Repetition is a staple for consistency in life. Begin each day by doing the following things.

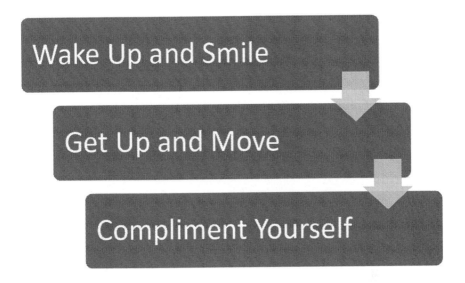

1. **Wake Up and Smile** – doing this sets the tone for your mood. It is important that you wake up feeling positive or you will succumb to the first negative encounter you have.

2. **Get Up and Move** – don't lounge around in the bed for too long after you awake. Remaining in bed gives you a moment to consider all that you must face and those things that brings sadness upon you. Once you get up, get moving.

3. **Compliment Yourself** – say something nice about yourself to enhance your mood or make you feel good. You should give yourself the first compliment of the day and carry yourself proudly wherever you go.

Self-Esteem Booster Cycle

You must create a cycle to boost your self-esteem. It is a never-ending cycle that keeps going and going. Whenever you feel down or defeated, repeat the words in the cycle. These are words of power and affirm the beliefs you should have about yourself.

The Lifestyle Enhancer

Your lifestyle will be greatly enhanced when positive things and acts are introduced into it. Think positively. Speak positively. Believe positively. Act positively. This assist you in doing what is necessary to enjoy a positive lifestyle without room or time for depression.

Replace all negative words and thoughts with all things positive. This is a necessary component of the healing process when depression strikes. Your life has purpose but you must live and believe this to be true.

Below is a cycle of positivity to help enhance your lifestyle. Familiarize yourself with the cycle and incorporate it into your daily style of living.

The Color Effect

The color effect is the process of exposing yourself to certain colors to help elevate or improve your mood. This is a positive channel in overcoming or defeating depression. It's not suggested that you decorate your living space in these colors only but to have them readily available in the moments you feel depressed.

The following colors have positive effects on your mood.

Blue is a color that is related to calmness. It helps you to feel relaxed and calm. The color also aides in decreasing blood pressure and producing clarity in the mind. Blue hues should be warm and not pastel to battle depression.

Yellow is a mood enhancing and invigorating color that energizes. Good energy is essential, as you attempt to battle depression. Embrace the color yellow in the early morning to set your mood for the day.

Green calms your anxiety and gives you a sense of reassurance about whatever is going on in your life. This color encourages tranquility. It also restores the mind and

Orange creates excitement and is great in motivating exercise. It's an upbeat color, so only focus on it when trying to get your energy levels up and not settle down.

Pink may not be a color that comes to mind when thinking of ways to enhance or improve your mood but it's a great one to do so. Exposure to this color settles the nerves and removes anxiety, anger and feelings of hostility.

Treatment for Depression

Anyone living with depression would prefer to treat themselves or find ways to get better without others knowing. While self-help is an option, it shouldn't be used without other resources as well. When executed properly, dynamic results can be gained from self-help techniques.

It is essential that those facing depression to be compassionate about their situation. To reach a state of compassion, you must initiate positive attributes in your life. Dealing with anxiety and stress can lead to suppressed feelings. Discover ways to help yourself feel and live better.

Self-Care

Along with therapy, research and a great support system, you should adapt a system of self-care to address your depression daily. This isn't a miracle approach but instead a sequence of individual choices that result in a healthy and positive lifestyle.

Here are a few self-care suggestions to implement into your daily regimen.

1. Begin Where You Are

It's ideal to escape to a serene location, the beach or spa to experience awesome self-care. However, you should begin by initiating the steps to taking care of yourself exactly where you are. At home, driving in your vehicle, on the job, out socializing and anywhere you find yourself are ideal places to give yourself the care you need. This requires the adaptation of skills or techniques that you can apply daily. Stop searching elsewhere for ways or remedies to help you feel good. Utilize the things or resources that are in your surroundings.

2. Shh! Your Body is Telling You Something

Get in tuned with what your body is saying to you. Of course, it's not speaking out loud but the body gives little hints about what is going on mentally, emotionally and physically. Depression drains you of all your energy and can cause headaches. Heart palpitations and increased sweating happen when anxiety sets in. Listening to your body when these things occur helps you to understand your mental state. Taking note of the symptoms helps you to initiate practices of self-care by preventing or avoiding the conditions that cause these problems.

3. Breathe Away Anxiety

Practice taking deep breaths multiple times a day. You can take these breaths at anytime and anyplace. When sitting at your desk – take a deep breath. On the drive home – take a deep breath. While waiting in line for coffee – take a deep breath. Anxiety often results in fast and shallow breaths. You begin to develop tension in certain muscles. Taking slow and deeply inhaled breaths is one way to fight through or battle anxiety attacks. This type breathing improves circulation, emits endorphins, and makes muscles less tense. It helps to practice the breathing exercises multiple times a day. Therefore, when anxiety or panic attacks set in, breathing will take little to no effort.

4. Love the Person Staring Back At You in the Mirror

Every morning and night, take a look in the mirror and identify at least one thing you love about yourself. Stop being so critical of yourself. This leads to a category of negative thoughts about why you are not good enough. Be kind to yourself and allow that kindness to begin with how you view yourself. Don't criticize your weight but instead, embrace your curves. Don't frown at your freckles but admire their uniqueness. Every asset about your body makes you unique in every way. Move now to take note of those areas in which you desire to see change, but don't think of them negatively. Focus on the motivations behind these changes.

5. Encourage Yourself

Speak positive affirmations to yourself. Don't speak negatively about yourself. The more negative thoughts you have about yourself, the more depression sets in. Eventually, your mind becomes a space that is clouded by negative judgement. To change or improve the way you speak about yourself, you must first recognize the issue. Stop putting yourself in timeout because you don't meet the standards of others. What will it take to make you happy? That is the important thought to focus on. Do and say things that encourage or motivate happiness in your life. Reward yourself for the little things by saying, "I really like the way I handled that" or "I tried and that's enough". These are among the most efficient things you can implement to alter your attitude towards yourself.

6. Go to Time-Out

Time-out isn't a punishment in this regard. It's a relief when anxiety or depression surfaces. It may be beneficial to take a break or step away when you begin to feel depressed or overly anxious. One of the most effective self-care tips is to walk away when the pressure begins to mount. Free yourself from any environment that is making you feel overwhelmed or sad. Simply excuse yourself by saying, "I need to step away for a quick second for a personal moment and will be back in ten." This permits you to care for yourself, while addressing those around you. A moment to yourself does wonders for your mental clarity. Your well-being must come first if your goal is to give the best part of yourself to others.

7. A Ten Minute Celebration

Sometimes you need to have a mini-celebration. Have

some fun just because. Depression makes you feel sad and uninterested. Therefore, you have no desire to do anything fun or exciting. Make a serious attempt to spend about ten minutes celebrating for no reason. Toast to the day. Eat cake and blow out the candles for no reason at all. Paint a picture and hang it on the wall at work or at home. These little spurts of fun or celebratory acts can lift your spirits or improve your mood in no time. You must try your best to accomplish this, especially on the days you don't feel up to it.

8. Adopt a Nighttime Routine

Depression makes falling asleep seem like a chore. Adapt a routine that clears your mind and prepares your body to rest comfortably through the night. Put your mobile devices on charge for the night. Shut down your computer or laptop. Enjoy a warm shower or bath. Sip tea or warm milk while reading or listening to soft music for about half-an-hour. Avoid intense or insensitive interactions. Doing these things places your mind in a relaxed state and makes getting to sleep easier.

Self-care is a vital part of your treatment routine for depression and anxiety. You must understand and know how to care for yourself before you can allow anyone else to do so. The professional approach is important but self-care is the complement that it needs to be most effective.

Do I Have Anxiety or Am I Depressed?

Many people are confused about their feelings in regards to feeling anxious or depressed. It works best if you are clear on how the two differ. In any case, if you are suffering with symptoms of either of the two, get a professional diagnosis and treatment advice.

Anxiety

Anxiety generates doubt and resistance about and towards things that are in the process of occurring. People who experience anxiety become anxious or afraid without reason and fear the unknown. A few common symptoms of anxiety include unwarranted sensations, withdrawal from unfamiliar people and places and overly protective of themselves.

You can teach yourself to deal with the symptoms of anxiety utilizing sensory techniques. This can alleviate your anxiety attacks altogether. It is iatrical that you teach yourself to observe and recognize the symptoms and ways to remain calm in all situations that usually make you anxious. Becoming anxious can irritate your body and kill your mood.

Why the Confusion?

Some people confuse the two because they may be taking medication for anxiety and also prescribed an anti-depressant. It is common for people to think they may be suffering from depression due to the medication. While this may sometimes be true, it doesn't happen in every case.

For instant relief from situations that cause anxiety, try these suggestions.

1. When anxiety sets in about an upcoming task such as an interview or exam

Study your best. Make sure that you've taken good notes and reviewed them carefully. Become as familiar as possible with the material. Think positive before engaging in the event. Smile, and embrace the opportunity to do great. This moment is a brief encounter and will not last your entire life.

2. When you feel anxiety setting in, BREATHE!

Assume a comfortable position. Sit in a quiet area with your eyes closed and inhale deeply, repeatedly. Hold your breath for about ten to fifteen seconds and release. Continue the exercise by engaging different areas of your body for the count. Squeeze your toes tightly for a few seconds, release. Tighten the muscles in your feet and ankles, release. Move upward and engage your calf muscles, release. You can do this until all the muscles of the body have been engaged. The act of inhaling will help you to feel better and should relieve you of your anxiety.

3. Kick anxious thoughts out of your mind

Once a thought enters your mind that causes you to become anxious, focus on a single phrase or color and say it repetitively. Try repeating the phrase, "it's okay, it's okay, it's okay" over an over until you believe it or that's the only thing your mind subconsciously hears. This works.

4. Hold your breath

Try holding your breath in for about six seconds. You'll begin to focus on breathing and not the thing that's causing you to be anxious. Be careful not to hold it too long.

5. Determine the exact thing that's causing the anxiety

If you are anxious about making an important decision, compose a list. List the positives and the cons. Think about them and move away from the negative thoughts that are causing you to feel anxious.

6. No Worry Zone

If you are becoming anxious or having panic attacks about things like war, terrorist attacks or the environment, let it go. You have no control over these things and are causing yourself worry and stress for no reason. If watching the news or reading the paper brings these things to your mind, stop watching and reading about them. Your sanity is important and clinging to negative news reports will only make the situation worse. Turn the television off or to another channel and if necessary, cancel your news subscription.

7. Avoid Anxiety Projects

If some projects make you anxious or feel overwhelmed, say no to them. Accept only those tasks or projects that you are comfortable embracing. You should never take on a project that brings anxious feelings to surface. Take control of your life and avoid negative or overwhelming tasks when possible.

8. Create a serene atmosphere

The atmosphere you're in has an impact on your anxiety levels. Add flowers to the room, turn on soft music and keep a clean space. This helps you to assume a state of relaxation and calmness in your environment.

9. Meditate

Resolving to a quiet and calm state helps you to forget the unbearable thoughts that plague your mind.

Meditate for about thirty minutes to clear your mind and focus on happy thoughts and feelings.

10. Go Outside

Get outside and breathe in the fresh air. Observe what you see while walking. Be mindful of the things around you to help you focus on that instead of what's making you feel anxious. Enjoy the calmness that the moment brings. This is a good step to help you regain control.

Following is a list of things many people experience during the onset of panic or anxiety episodes.

- Rapid heartbeat
- Feelings of terror or upcoming death
- Afraid of going insane
- Feelings of choking or being choked
- Shaking uncontrollably
- Hard time breathing
- Suddenly becomes faint or dizzy
- Queasiness
- Sweats
- Detachment from others or reality
- Tightness in the chest
- Tingling sensation

The Exercise

Circle the symptoms above as they apply to you when feeling anxious.

Next, rate your level of worry or concern about having another episode: 1 – no worries to 5 – extremely worried.

Also, rate your level of discomfort during the attacks: 1 – not uncomfortable to 5 – extremely uncomfortable.

Lastly, the final question: has anxiety caused you to change your actions or behavior such as avoiding areas or circumstances that you think will cause an attack or no longer visit places where one is likely to occur?

---

*If you rank levels 3 or higher to the first two questions, you should implement exercises to help you overcome your anxiety. If you are avoiding places or situations due to fear of an attack, you are giving in to the fear associated with anxiety.

The Anxiety Factor

While professional help is available for anxiety, it can often be controlled with simple strategies and self-control techniques. This is more of a feeling than an emotional state. The onset of anxiety can set-in quickly and without warning. Make an effort to observe and identify the causes or situations that cause you to feel anxious. The factor is what triggers your anxiety and the steps you can implement to calm anxiousness and eliminate that factor. You are the common denominator in each of the factors. The task at hand is for you to establish a serene moment the instant anxiety kicks in.

The following strategies may be useful in helping you to overcome whatever it is that ignites your anxieties.

Strategy #1: Pour Out the Soda

Coffee may be a great start to your day, but say goodbye to those afternoon sodas. Caffeine, the high fructose corn syrup and other chemicals it contains can disturb the central nervous system. Anxiety triggers nerves and if they are already amped up on caffeine, you'll find yourself in greater distress.

Strategy #2: Iron Out Your Budget

Many people are up late hours of the night trying to determine ways to improve their finances. You will begin to stress and experience bouts of anxiety if your budget is not clean. Get ahead of your finances. Begin by stopping the unnecessary spending and start saving where and whenever possible. Track your budget for a few weeks and decide what areas can be trimmed more. This will help to alleviate some of the anxiety that your finances bring into your life.

Saving Tips

- Cancel your cable and sign up for something less expensive
- Select a less expensive mobile plan
- Ask for a lower interest rate on your credit cards
- Cancel your newspaper and magazine subscriptions

Strategy #3: Explore for a Day

Getting away from your usual surroundings will help you to free your mind and relax a bit. Plan a little exploration for the day to visit someplace quiet and comforting. You don't have to go far or you may choose to go as far away as possible. The point is to just escape the usual and connect with something peaceful.

Strategy #4: Fall In Love with Lavender

There are several healing and relaxing agents in lavender. Use it to calm you and coax your anxieties.

Add it to your anxiety eliminating kit and you'll feel more relaxed during the day and night.

- Add a few drops to your bath for a calming sensation. Infuse your bath with leaves of lavender to appease tight muscles or aching joints.
- Place the essential oil on a cotton ball and place underneath your pillow to enjoy a peaceful night's rest.
- Add it to a diffuser to help you sleep.
- Massage it into your temple to relieve headaches.
- Use it for back or muscle massages.

All the above uses of lavender offer calming and soothing effects, which are useful in battling anxiety.

Professional Treatment for Depression

In moments of depression, it seems as if you're sinking and will never rise above water. It may feel like the end is near, but there are treatment options to get you through the toughest moments. If you are living with depression and aren't getting the most enjoyment from your life, you should seek treatment from a professional.

What treatment options are available?

Because depression has a different face for everyone it effects, treatment options will vary among patients. One person may benefit from "Type A" treatment, while someone else may not experience the same benefit. Therefore consulting a professional for an individual diagnosis is always the best idea.

Treatment Advice

Get to know depression. Familiarize yourself with the causes of depression. Find out if it is due to an existing medical ailment you have. Treat that condition before dealing with the depression. However, your depression will need immediate attention also. If you suffer from severe depression, you will respond best to extreme treatment.

Trust the process for successful progress. Your care provider may not be able to initiate a treatment plan immediately. A discovery process may be needed. This is the time taken to observe your condition closely and develop possible treatment options. In some cases, you may have to undergo a few sessions before finding an effective treatment plan.

Nurture social connections. Take care of your social circle and nourish them, as they help to shield you from episodes of depression.

Give it time. You didn't develop depression overnight and it won't go away overnight. Allow time for your treatment process to take effect. You may feel that it's taking too much time or even that it's not working but remember it's a process. There will be moments of frustration and extreme sadness even during treatment. However, an effective program will help you overcome your depression with time.

Psychotherapy

If your depression does not stem from an existing medical condition, you could possibly talk it out with a therapist and experience good results. The skills and techniques developed in therapy are designed to give you the tools to work through the issues that causes the depression in the first place. This approach prepares you to defeat the illness and prevent it from reoccurring.

Various types of therapy are available. Among the most common are cognitive behavioral, psychodynamic and interpersonal therapies. In many cases, the three can be combined for more precise results.

Some therapy options incorporate real-world strategies and teach patients to recondition their thought process and to execute behavioral techniques to beat depression. Therapy is ideal for helping you to identify and approach the source of your depression. You understand what triggers it and how to confront or alleviate those triggers to begin living a more fulfilled and less stressful life.

Clear the Smoke Screen

Therapy is designed to not only treat your depression but to help you understand what causes it to surface. When depressed, a cloudy feeling overcomes you, and it feels as if you're living blind. Therapy helps you clear the smoke screen and see the things that effect you most in like.

Relationship dynamics. You must understand the dynamic of your relationships in order to build more solid and rewarding ones. The goal is to make the current ones better, decrease isolation and establish social connections to avoid depression.

Establishing healthy guidelines. Being stress and confused sometimes causes you to make bad choices and decisions. This includes accepting tasks or doing favors that you really aren't comfortable or capable of doing. Therapy teaches you that there is a comfort zone where no is an acceptable response. Your "yes" has brought you major stress and is likely contributing to your feeling of overwhelm

Dealing with the issues of life. Speaking with a professional can give you good feedback or insight on the best ways to deal with the obstacles and challenges that life brings.

Individual and Group Treatment Options

Once you decide to go to therapy, your perception may be sitting on a couch or in a chair across from the therapist sharing your feelings. While this is the perfect description of individual therapy, group therapy is an option and paints a different perspective. Both are extremely effective when utilized properly and offer different advantages.

Individual therapy allows you to share your most intimate experiences or issues with only one person, your therapist. All the attention is directed to you and your issues. The plan is devised to accommodate only you for the time that you are in session.

Group therapy is somewhat different. You are listening and sharing. You listen to a group of peers who have similar issues with depression as they share their experiences. The focus is on the group and not just an individual. In addition, you can grow from what others have gone through and possibly prevent similar things from happening in your situation. Group sessions expose you to some people who have battled and beat depression. They may be utilizing the group to assist in their recovery to prevent a relapse.

Power in the Pyramid

Choosing a Therapist

Your therapist should be someone you are comfortable sharing the most private details of your condition with. This should be a person who is trained to listen and devise an effective approach or strategy to teach you to overcome your issues. This person will be supportive and tuned in to your needs.

There are several routes to locating the right therapist.

- Listen to the thoughts and suggestions of others. Speak with friends, family and others about their experiences with mental counselors. They can provide insight on which ones to consider and which ones to avoid.
- Your primary physician can provide a list of referrals.
- Cost-efficient options are available through local health centers, religious organizations and community facilities that provide mental healthcare.

Alternative Options

Alternative treatment options are available via the use of OTC or herbal supplements. While there is no scientific data to support that supplements are effective treatment for depression, if the symptoms you exhibit are because of an insufficiency of nutrients, vitamins may work as a complement to the treatment you are receiving.

Please note that supplements can cause side effects or interact with prescription medications. Always consult with your primary care provider and therapist before beginning an alternative treatment for depression.

You Can Help

It is desirable that friends and family provide support for those dealing with depression. One of the worst parts of living with depression is having to go through the struggle alone. Unfortunately, helping someone work through depression has its pros and cons. It can cause a toll on the supporter if you fail to take care of your own needs. You can easily become so consumed with the problems someone else is facing that you begin to feel overwhelmed and stressed yourself. To offer strong support, take care of yourself on all levels.

Behind the Sadness

Depression is a severe illness that impacts the lives of people around the globe. It changes the lives of people of all ages each day. Life undergoes dramatic overhauls when depression sets in. If a person is depressed, there friends and loved ones will be effected in some capacity.

If you know someone who is living with depression, you are probably experiencing a category of motions yourself. You may be feeling angry because you have no idea why this happening. You may feel guilty because you didn't realize it had gotten this bad. You may even feel sad because you see your loved one suffering and aren't sure what you should do to help. All these are normal emotions to have. Helping someone cope with depression can be challenging. And if you neglect yourself, it will become overwhelming.

Know that there are ways you can help. It starts with learning, understanding and listening. Learn any details you can on what your friend is going through. Understand what depression is and how it impairs their life. Listen to your loved one as they share their feelings and experiences. Remember to think about yourself and what you need throughout the process. Taking care of your needs is not selfish. It is necessary. You can only be a good support option if you are emotionally strong.

The Language of Depression

Depression is severe. Don't assume that depression comes with a switch and can be turned on and off. It's a severe condition that depletes a person's energy, determination and outlook on life. It's not possible to just tell depression to take a hike and it disappears.

Depression changes people. People who suffer from depression lead an impaired life. They can't connect with those they love like they once did. They speak out of tone and often with frustration or haste. Keep in mind, this is not the person you love talking. It's the depression.

You can't cover it up. As much as you would like, you can't make depression be something it isn't. It's not a pretty picture and it isn't something you can put away when it's inconvenient. Be honest about the problem and encourage them to acknowledge that they have an issue of depression.

You're support and not the fixer. Your goal should be to offer support and love. Don't place blame and don't attempt to diagnose the root or source of the issue. The road to recovery is one that can only be traveled by the person who is depressed. You are simply along for the ride.

How to Identify the Symptoms

In many cases, friends and family will notice that a

loved one is depressed before the person notices that something is wrong. Therefore, it is crucial that you know what the signs of depression are when you see them.

Concerns should be raised if...

The person isn't the same anymore. They may have little to no interest in work, school, family or other social events. They may have become withdrawn and uninterested in things that they once enjoyed.

They see everything negative in their life. This can be extremely sad to watch, as the person thinks that they have no hope and everything in life is hopeless.

Constantly complains of headaches and frequent pains. You may hear the person complain of stomach aches, pain in the joints and other areas. They will often say that they are fatigued and overwhelmed.

The person is not sleeping the way they usually do. If the sleep pattern is disturbed to where they are sleeping more or less than usual, depression may be the reason.

Eating habits are extremely different. If you observe that your loved one isn't eating as they should or eating excessively more than usual, depression could be the reason.

The Conversation

The challenge exists in know what to say to your loved one. It can be hard to bring the subject up or figuring out where to begin. You have no idea how they will accept or react to your approach.

Here are a few suggestions to help you know where to begin. Keep in mind that you should be compassionate throughout the entire process. You may be surprised to know how much a simple conversation will help a person dealing with depression.

There will be no easy end to the problem even after having a conversation. People who are depressed will always resort to isolation and you must continue to be supportive and persistent in assisting that they get professional help immediately.

The Conversation Starter

I'm growing concerned about you.
I've noticed a few changes in you and hoping all is well with you.
I'm checking up on you. I noticed you've seemed sad recently.

The Questions

How long have you had these feelings?
What took place to bring about your feelings?
What can I do to support your needs at the time?
Have you looked into seeking help?

Things You Can Say

You don't have to face this by yourself. I will be here for you.
It may seem impossible but the emotions you're having will get better.
I have never experienced what you're feeling but I want to help you.

If you feel like giving up, hold on just another second for however long you can and call me.
You mean so much to me. I need you here with me.
Let me know what it is you need from me and I'll do it.

Avoid Saying These Type Things

You're imagining things.
Everyone has problems like this.
Look at the positive side.
Your life is great. What makes you want to end it?
I can't change your circumstance.
Just get over it.
Why are you acting this way?
Shouldn't you be over this by now?

In The Event of a Crisis

You may not believe that your loved one is even considering taking their own life. Depression causes people to think about and do things they wouldn't under ordinary circumstances. Their judgement is impaired and thoughts are unclear during depression, which causes them to believe that death is their only way out.

Suicide is extremely common among those who suffer with depression. It is crucial that you can identify the warning signs.

- Speaking of ending their life or hurting themselves.
- Displaying signs of hopelessness
- Acting out or being self-destructive
- Settling their affairs and preparing to say goodbye to everyone
- Trying to find pills, knives or guns
- All of sudden becomes calm following a serious episode of depression

If you feel that a friend or family member is living with depression and contemplating suicide, speak with them about those concerns immediately. The topic may be uncomfortable or difficult to approach but it will be the best way you can help them and possibly save your loved one's life. Talk to them and encourage them to talk to a professional immediately.

Encourage Them to See a Professional

You have no control over the process of another person's recovery process but you can suggest that they get help. It can be challenging to convince them to seek assistance from a professional. When someone is depressed, their energy is at level 0 and the idea of setting an appointment to see someone can actually seem like a lot. In many regards, the person feels lost and that they can't be helped. In some ways, they may feel abandoned or that no one is there for them.

It requires a little effort and persistency to convince your loved one that they have an underlying condition. Help them to see that it is possible to get over their illness with help.

If they deny there is a problem or don't want to seek counsel:

Encourage them to visit their doctor. They may be reluctant to see a mental health professional but willing to see someone they are more familiar with, such as their doctor. The physician can perform tests to eliminate the possibility that a medical issue is making them depressed. After this diagnosis, he can make a professional recommendation for your loved one to see a professional counselor.

Tell the depressed person that you'll assist them in the search for a therapist and even accompany them to their consultation. It may be hard to find a therapist in the beginning. The process is not a quick one. Keep in mind that your loved one is likely tired and frustrated and won't be very cooperative throughout the process. Provide help by calling around and checking available resources.

Ask your loved one to write a list of any symptoms they have for the doctor to review. Be sure to add anything you've observed as well. Remind them to write down how they feel at various times of the day.

Give Them the Support They Need

Your biggest role throughout the entire process is to be the support your loved one needs. Offer your unbiased ear and unwavering love during the treatment. You must be compassionate and try to remain calm when they become negative or lash out at you. It's all a part of the coping and treatment process.

Be the help they need. Assist your loved one in making the important decisions and moving forward to make and attend all appointments. Conduct intense research and help them stick to the guidelines of the program.

Remain realistic. Seeing your loved one go through this is hard to watch. It is essential that you exercise extreme patience. The treatment will take a while and the recovery will take longer. Remain steadfast and there for them.

Be a good example. You can be the example by demonstrating the proper way to lead a healthy life. Eat well. Get plenty of rest and stay clear of substances.

Convince them to become active. Don't just tell your loved one to go out for a walk, invite them to join you. Schedule a date to a movie or out to dinner. Physical activity is extremely beneficial. Therefore, try your best to motivate them to move around. Taking short or long walks in a group or with a friend should be the easiest thing to convince them to do. They may be reluctant at first. Express that you understand but don't quit trying.

Help out wherever possible. You probably notice that your loved one is struggling to tackle simple tasks. Help out with the little things whenever you can. Don't overwhelm yourself but maybe suggest that you both tackle the task together.

Anxiety and Panic Attacks: Know the Difference

Your emotions are high and nerves all over the place. Immediately you begin to notice sweaty hands, armpits and possibly face. The trembles have taken over your body, and suddenly you feel nauseous. It's one of the most uncomfortable feelings you've ever experienced and it's extremely frightening because you have no idea what's going on.

Could it be an anxiety attack or perhaps a panic attack? How can you tell the difference? Are you sure that there is a difference? Chances are, you are experiencing either a panic attack or anxiety. These are both a state of emotions but extremely different from each other.

Anxiety is described as an emotion that involves persistent or constant worry about a circumstance or impending occurrence such as sickness or the passing of a loved one. This include little things like an interview or how something will turn out. Signs that you are suffering from anxiety may include hypervigilance, irritability and tiredness. These conditions have the potential to be chronic.

Panic attacks are small spurts of concentrated fear, usually identified by rapid heart rate, short-lived chest pain or shallow breath. These episodes typically last less than half-an-hour and can happen once or repetitively and often for no reason at all. Some sufferers rush to the hospital because they fear what is happening to them is a heart attack.

The Anxiety vs. Panic Attack Difference Factor

Anxiety is what one go through because of extreme worry about an upcoming event or engagement. They worry that the outcome or end result will be negative. Usually tension or tightening of the muscles accompany anxiety with extreme unrest. The onset is typically a gradual one.

Panic attacks are not anxiety. They are unforeseen bouts of penetrating fright due to something taking place at that very moment. It ignites a fight-or-flight reaction that our minds are conditioned to have in cases of sudden danger. There's an alarm that sounds and our bodies react with immediate fear.

Some people may experience both emotions simultaneously.

Panic Attack vs. Anxiety Comparison Chart	
Riding your bike along a dark trail and you think something bad is about to happen	Anxiety
Riding your bike along a dark trail and a dog jumps out and attacks you	Panic attack
Walking to your car after work and you worry that someone is waiting by your car to abduct you	Anxiety

Panic Attack vs. Anxiety Comparison Chart	
Walking to your car after work and someone runs up behind you to grab your bag	Panic attack

*Anxiety is what takes place when you fear something bad will occur.
*Panic attacks take place when something bad suddenly occurs.

Treatment of Panic Attacks or Anxiety

The mind is programmed to experience either or both of these emotional states. Some people worry more due to their fragile nervous system. If they are around or raised by individuals who constantly worry, they usually follow or learn the same pattern.

Professionally, more individuals seek clinical help due to anxiety than panic attacks. This is primarily because anxiety is a common emotion that many witness in everyday life. It is sometimes more difficult to control and exists in numerous situations or circumstances.

Those who live a life filled with consistent uneasiness and anxiety about several or mounting situations are typically categorized with general anxiety. This group is treated with an approach that teaches them to control their worry and fears. It can be done by challenging or confronting their lingering fears and encouraging them to improve their tolerance in conditions of ambiguity which is a large part of the anxious feelings that surface.

The approach or treatment for panic attacks may include a diagram or presentation that makes clear the fight-or-flight reaction. The mind is working to assist them during this time. Once a person has experienced a panic attack, they tend to avoid anything or situation that spikes adrenaline. You learn to hyperventilate controllably for a few seconds to overcome whatever fear is lingering. You are taught to internalize those instances that are fearful and learn how to soothe them.

Treatment doesn't eliminate or make these disorders disappear completely but it teaches you how to overcome both in the moment. The extent and effectiveness of treatment is based on the severity of each condition.

Panic Attack Indicators

Trembles
Cold sweats
Swimming of the head
Abdominal tightness
Rapid heart beat
Fear of death
Hot flashes

Warning

It can be difficult to tell if a person is having a heart attack or a panic attack because the symptoms are similar. Ask them if they suffer from panic attacks or have had one before. If the answer is no, it is best to seek emergency care to rule out the possibility of a heart attack.

Anxiety Indicators

Restlessness
Consistent Worry
Anxious Feelings
Inability to Focus
Tiredness
Extremely Irritable
Interruption of Sleep Patterns

Anxiety Reducers

It is possible to decrease or reduce anxiety. Following of few of these habits may assist in doing so and help you to feel better overall.

- Consume a well-balanced diet – eat food that is abundant in fiber, protein and nutrients. Add vegetables, fish, whole grains and high-protein meats to the diet.
- Probiotics – foods with probiotics serve as a great source for contributing to positive mental health.
- Minimum Caffeine Intake – absorbing excessive amounts of caffeine can make you feel nervous or jittery, which can heighten the occurrence of anxiety.
- Say NO to Alcohol. Alcohol is strongly associated to disorders of anxiety. If you experience them often, you should abstain from the consumption of alcoholic beverages.
- No Nicotine – smoking is linked to an enhanced risk of encountering anxiety disorders.
- Get Physically Active – exercising regularly is good for mental clarity and helps to establish a decreased risk of getting a disorder like anxiety. It may not be enough to help someone who has

already been diagnosed but works to decrease the chances of acquiring the disorder.

- Meditation/Yoga – both have been researched and appear to decrease symptoms for individuals who have been diagnosed with or treated for anxiety.

Social Anxiety

It is common for people to become nervous or feel insecure during stressful events such as public speaking occasions and job interviews. However, social anxiety is not just a feeling of extreme nervousness. This disorder causes you to fear being embarrassed in social situations. It can become so intense that you begin to exercise extreme measures just to avoid going certain places or doing certain things.

Regardless of how intensely shy a person may be, they can work through their issues and overcome their feelings of awkwardness in social settings and resume a normal life.

Why Does Social Anxiety Happen?

You may feel like you're the only one living with this issue but you're not. People all over the world deal with social anxiety each day. It causes them to be extremely uncomfortable and miss out on a lot of social events and activities. While many people are impacted by the disorder, their triggers are often quite different.

This type of anxiety usually takes place in social settings. Sometimes, it is connected to a certain social setting, such as mingling with new people, attending parties or appearing in front of a large crowd.

Here are a few common triggers:

- Encountering new people
- Engaging in chatty conversation
- Public engagements
- On stage appearances
- Being at the forefront of a major event
- Being mocked or condemned
- Communicating with people of importance
- Being selected to answer questions or give demonstrations
- Dating someone new
- Speaking out in a crowd
- Tests
- Using the restroom away from home
- Dining out in public
- Talking on the phone with people you don't know
- Attending social events or outings

Signs to Look For In the Disorder

If your nerves get rattled in social environments, it doesn't necessarily indicate that you have the disorder. It is ordinary for people to feel a little nervous or shy during some occasions. However, it doesn't prevent them from functioning as usual and getting out into the world mingling with others.

It is common for someone to get butterflies before speaking to a group of individuals. However, if it is social anxiety, the worry sets in long before the event. You may come up with all types of excuses to avoid attending. If you show up, you may begin to tremble while speaking or break out in a cold sweat.

Emotional Indicators

Extreme worry and nervousness in any social setting
Continuous worry leading up to an event but weeks or months prior to it taking place
Constant worry that someone is watching you or passing judgement, even from strangers
Worrying that you'll be embarrassed by something you do
Scared someone will sense that you're afraid or nervous

Physical Indicators

Change in color in the face
Shallow breathing
Nauseous feeling
The shakes
Rapid heartbeat
Sweats or growing extremely warm
Dizziness

Behavioral Indicators

So fearful of social engagements that it interrupts your life
Blending into the background and not associating at social events to prevent embarrassment
Afraid to attend events alone or go anywhere without someone being by your side
Drinking to get your mind off what you have to do

Overcoming the Disorder

While it appears that social anxiety is something that you will have to live with all your life, there are tools to help you overcome it. It begins with stimulating your mental composition.

Those who battle social anxiety often experience negative feelings and thought processes that stimulate their worries and nerves. They have these type thoughts:

- I will only end up embarrassing myself.
- I'll sound funny when I open my mount to speak and everyone will laugh.
- They'll all see m as crazy.
- I have no idea to say and they'll be bored with me.

Confronting any negative thoughts is the best way to defeat your feelings of anxiety.

1. **Pinpoint those thoughts that aggravate your nervousness in social encounters or engagements.** For instance, if you have concerns about an event that will take place, you may begin to worry that you will do or say something to ruin it. People will say you are hopeless.

2. **Assess and contest all negative thoughts.**

You should not just accept the thoughts that surface in your head. Double guess them. Ask yourself if you are sure that things will work out the way your mind is telling you. Thinking logically or analyzing the situation closely can help you formulate more realistic thoughts. This approach helps you to put positive thoughts in place of the negative ones that are overshadowing your mind.

It can make you feel extremely awkward to think of the reasons behind all the negative feelings you have. However, understanding why you have these thoughts will help to reduce the impact these factors have on your quality of life.

3. Concentrate on other people in attendance.

When attending social events and your nerves are rattled, it's easy to become consumed or overwhelmed with your thoughts. It is simple to have a passing or lingering thought that someone may be staring or passing judgement on you. In the meantime, you are concentrating on the reactions of your body. You think that you can control the jitters and the sweaty armpits. Paying such close attention to yourself only intensifies your anxiety. It also removes you from the moment and prevents you from being able to experience the moment fully.

Focus on things going on around you more than you focus on yourself. This helps to decrease those feelings of anxiety that creep in from nowhere. The more attention you give the people and things happening around you, the less focus you'll direct towards what may go wrong with you.

4. Stay in control of those breaths.

Anxiety causes tremendous changes to occur in the body. Initially, you'll begin to feel like you're losing your breath. Breathing too heavily or hyperventilating can interfere with carbon dioxide and oxygen levels in the body. This can cause other symptoms such as rapid heartbeat, dizziness and anxiety.

Taking slow deep breaths can help to control your anxiety.

5. Confront your worries

It helps to identify and confront the things that worry you most about social engaging. Confronting them is better than ignoring them or pretending they don't exist. Pretending your fears don't exist only makes things escalate further out of control. While avoiding a situation makes you comfortable in the moment, the stress and fear you endure leading up to it can be life-altering. The more afraid of a situation you are, the bigger your problem becomes.

Take small steps and don't try to confront all your fears at once. Exercise patience and remain calm. Don't give up if it takes longer to confront a particular fear. What you should be proud of is that you are making an effort to overcome it.

Life and Happiness After Depression

The turmoil and anguish that depression takes you through is more than some can withstand. It takes a great deal of courage, patience and resilience to get to and go through the treatment process. After months and sometimes years of treatment, you are finally at the recovery stage. Life is more comfortable and you have more hope now than ever before. While things are better, you may still have feelings of discomfort because of your experiences.

What happens throughout the process? How do you cope or get through each day once you've identified the problem and sought treatment? The answers to these questions will vary among individuals but it's important to realize that your life can be of great quality once you have overcome depression.

The Difference Factor

Research shows that one of the greatest contributing factors to healthy living after depression is a solid support system. It's crucial to have friends or family that are by your side during the entire process.

If you are close with a depressed person, you probably harbor feelings of loneliness and think that you are not making a big difference in their situation. Those who stuck around and offered love and support are a big part of the reason that the person was able to overcome their depression. In many cases, when most people get through their depression, they participate in increased physical activity and spiritual exercises during recovery.

Recovery Aides

Even after you've been in treatment for a while or possibly ended treatment, continue to practice self-care, remain actively engaged and stay physically active. Doing so keeps you healthy and happy. Your process of healing isn't one that will occur overnight. It requires a lifetime commitment because depression can return at any time. It takes a strong mental capacity to continue with life during and after depression.

Time Makes No Difference

You may be surprised to learn that a person can

enter into complete recovery regardless of how long they've lived with it. A person may have suffered from depression for one month or one year and return to full mental health.

It doesn't matter if your depression has been under control for three months or three years. Keep the proper relationships active to avoid returning to a life of uncontrollable thoughts and emotions.

1. Stay Connected with friends, family and therapist. These are the people that care and want to see you be happy and full of life. Maintain contact and arrange for an occasional meeting to get out and enjoy lunch or just good conversation.

2. Talk about your feelings. Depression no longer rules your life. You are in control of your feelings and have every right to let others know how you feel. Talk openly and honestly about how your emotions are these days. Let them know how you feel after certain interactions or conversations.

3. Embark on the things that bring you the most joy. Get out and enjoy your friends and family. Make new friends and create new experiences. You have spent too long living in depression. You may have difficulty accepting that you deserve happiness.

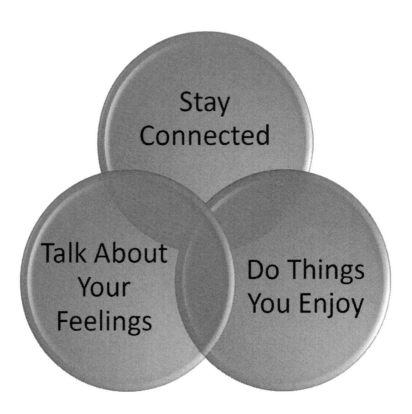

The Happy Life

Your life becomes one of happiness once you overcome depression. It's up to you to create and sustain the happiness in your life. There will be constant reminders that you were once unable to function as a normal human being. It's okay. These are only reminders and no longer triggers. The tools you gained in treatment help you move forward with confidence.

Here are a couple tips to help you resume and continue a life of happiness.

- Continue with therapy. You may feel better and like yourself again but don't stop attending your therapy sessions. You may be able to attend group sessions instead of individual therapy once you reach the recovery phase.

- Don't be afraid to talk about what you went through. It helps to discuss the struggles you faced. This is a clear sign that you are over it and not ashamed of what happen in your life.

These tips can help you achieve true happiness once you've dealt with your depression issues. Keep them in mind and use them often.

Adapt the Following Types of Interests:

Constructive – these activities help present a category of pride. This activity leads to doing works or activities at the house. Complete a task or a project or learn a new skill. Study a course or take a class that you find interesting.

Pleasurable – these activities are those that bring joy to your heart. They can be done for fun and excitement. You will feel a sense of relaxation after enduring pleasurable activities.

Altruistic – these activities offer companionship and receive extreme appreciation from others. You spend time helping others and trying to help their lives feel fulfilled. This type of activity delivers happiness to the life and spirt.

It is difficult to battle depression if you don't keep busy. It helps to engage socially and keep busy during productive. Your ultimate goal to happiness is to make every effort to be well-poised in life events. Engage socially, intellectually and culturally. Identify your priorities and make the necessary adjustments to align them with your life. If small issues arise, take small steps to solve them. Don't allow them to overwhelm you and feel free to reach out for help if needed. Avoid those habits that once caused you to feel sad or worthless. Your life is important and it is imperative that you understand your worth.

Begin and end each day with the following affirmations.

Life is great and I'm excited about my future.

Every obstacle ahead of me is one that I can overcome.

My biggest fear is that I will not have the chance to accomplish the one thing that scares me most.

I am valuable and I am needed.

I love my life!

Imprint